Praise for

Become an
AMAZING
Coach

"If you are a coach, considering coaching, or looking at ways to impact a person's life by more than just helping them perfect their craft within the sport, this is a book for you. The true benefit of a coach comes from being able to help an athlete become a better version of themselves within the sport and in life. This book gives you insights on how to do this and much more."

Chuck Kemeny—Executive Level Coach
LifeSport Coaching

"Fear can be paralyzing and can keep you from becoming the person you dream to be. Morgon takes you through his coaching journey and shows you how to take that first step towards your own pathway to becoming a coach. *Become an Amazing Coach* transforms the reader's passion and dreams into confidence and success."

Bill Brenner—Chief Operating Officer
U.S. Masters Swimming

"If you want to start a fire, you need a spark. Meet your spark. Morgon is a mentor, a partner, a pusher, a planner. Morgon is an amazing coach and his words will inspire you to be an amazing coach too. Your expertise is ready to be shared with the community around you—to build, to inspire, and to move people! The passion to share is the passion that drives Morgon, and you can feel that in every word of this book. Enjoy this read and get out and go!"

Earl Walton—Global Director
Training and Coaching IRONMAN

"Morgon breaks the book down into easy digestible chapters to understand the fire in the belly to be a coach to others. Couldn't put this book down because I can relate so well as to what I look for in a 70.3 Ironman coach. The energy flew off the pages and left every page more positive. I don't know how that is possible!"

Rhonda Vetere—EVP Global Chief
Information Officer, Herbalife Nutrition

"Regardless of whether you're coaching athletes to a new personal record, or coaching software engineers to create the next best thing, people are always at the core. Morgon's amicable nature and infectious positivity make people want to be around him and listen to what he has to say. He understands how to unearth what really drives people and what might be in the way of their goals, but Morgon's true superpower is simply caring for people.

Morgon's voice and booming smile resonate throughout the pages of this book. He provides insight on how he's built an extremely successful coaching practice and some hard lessons learned along the way. His easy writing style feels more like a conversation than reading a book. If you're new to coaching or trying to get better, this book has everything you need. Spoiler alert—Treating athletes like humans and seeing them for who they are is rule number one!"

Jody Fletcher—Executive Coach
e5 Professional Coaching

Confidence Lessons Publishing

Become an
AMAZING
Coach

Morgon Latimore

The first step
is to believe
it's possible.

To request permissions, contact the author at
CoachMorgon@LPureCoaching.com

Paperback ISBN: 978-1-952313-04-2
Ebook ISBN: 978-1-952313-05-9

Printed in the United States of America

Edited by Danielle Radden and Shannon Waters
Cover Art by Danielle Radden
Layout by Danielle Radden
Foreword by Alyson Watson

Confidence Lessons Publishing
www.ConfidenceLessonsPublishing.com

I would like to dedicate this book to my grandmother, Estella Latimore, who is gone but still a part of everything I accomplish.

Table of Contents

The first step
is to believe
it's possible.

Foreword

By Alyson Watson

What does it mean to be an amazing coach?

This is a weighty question. I have had the benefit of having many different coaches throughout my life—some great and some not-so-great. It is easy to identify a great coach in the moment, but what are those important qualities? I'd like to share with you a story about a recent experience I had with a truly amazing coach that will help bring to life some of the key points in the book you are about to read.

I am a competitive triathlete. Despite coming to the sport later in life, I have enjoyed some success—qualifying for both the half and full Ironman world championships, and even setting a bike course record at an inaugural Ironman 70.3 race. I am highly motivated, and I just truly enjoy the long hours of training. That's why it was so difficult and confusing when I just couldn't seem to summon any enthusiasm to train earlier this spring. It was like the little internal fire always pushing me forward had gone out. I reached out to my coach for help, but I really felt it was my responsibility to find that drive and motivation again. I was lost.

Morgon and I have been friends for some time. He is not my coach, but I have watched in awe as he has conquered the most challenging ultra-endurance events, and further expanded his athlete-centered coaching philosophy, while projecting a positive and upbeat attitude even under the most challenging circumstances. Somehow sensing that I was in a rut, Morgon reached out to me a few months ago just to see how I was doing. I told him I was struggling a bit, and he asked me, "What is your why?" This question caught me completely off guard.

One of the most moving books I have read in recent years is Simon Sinek's *Start with Why*, and I am a firm believer that everything we do should be rooted in a deep understanding of our why. Still, at that moment, I struggled to answer this basic question. Hearing my difficulty, Morgon scheduled a phone call with me to talk through the issues I was facing and to help me reconnect with my deeper motivations. During our call, I found myself teary-eyed as I explained to him what truly motivates me as a person, and where I derive my energy and passion. We discussed everything from my childhood to my work, the major stressors and joys of my life, and how I am working to better align my external life with my internal motivations. I am at a crossroads both personally and professionally. Morgon helped me to see that, while I have made progress toward developing a more fulfilling life, I was stagnating again. Without intentional action, I would continue down a path that would move me further from the source of my energy and happiness.

He ended the call by giving me a reading and writing assignment (Imagine giving your friend an assignment? Yep, that's Morgon!), and scheduled a follow-up phone call. I did my homework and read the book. Twice. It was precisely what I had needed. My training improved almost immediately. I felt more secure and in control of my life and direction. My energy and attitude improved, and I was back in a place to effect positive change and actively direct the course of my life. Morgon has continued to schedule check-ins with me, and continued to give me assignments— each one helping to reignite the fire that I thought I had lost.

Which brings me to the book you are about to read: one of my dreams is to one day be a coach myself. The reason I would like to coach is because the thing that brings me the most joy in this world is helping others to see that they are limitless, and that any limitations they perceive exist only in their own minds. Triathlon helped me learn this for myself, and that realization has been transformative in all aspects of my life. I want to help others to experience this same powerful transformation and watch their dreams take flight. Despite the personal success I have had, and despite reading every book on endurance training that I can get my hands on, I have hesitated to make the leap into coaching because I felt that I do not have enough experience, and I just don't quite know where to begin. I shared this with Morgon in one of our early phone calls, and he let me read an early draft of this book. By the time I reached Chapter 6, I knew that I could be a great coach. Coaching is part of my future. This book gave me the confidence to invest in a coaching certification course and begin my path toward becoming an amazing coach, with Morgon as a mentor. This book gave me the tools I needed to take a big step forward in my own life, and I know it can do the same for you.

I will close with this: during one of our phone calls, I asked Morgon why he was taking this time to help me. He responded simply that this is what he does. His gift and his passion are helping people realize their full potential, express their gifts, and live more fulfilled lives. Morgon truly cares about people. This is precisely what makes him an amazing coach. While it is true that Morgon is not my coach in the traditional sense— he does not write my training plans nor help me with specific aspects of training— he is teaching me to build a happier, more fulfilled, and more present life, every day. Read this book, trust your instincts, believe in your abilities, move in the direction that you are called, and enjoy your journey. The world needs more amazing coaches, and you have come to the right place!

Become an
AMAZING
Coach

Introduction

In the beginning of any epic journey, we must decide how we will start. This single choice will set the foundation for future choices. There are always choices—we don't always make the ones that we love, but they still need to be made. Then there are those choices that we wish we would have made, but never did. We reflect on the past and wonder what could have been. It's like going over to your friend's house for a barbecue. When it is time to leave, they ask you if you want to take a plate home. You decline, trying to be polite, but once you get home you wish you would have said yes to the plate, because now you are starving. Damn choices got you again!

Why are choices so hard? Because life is hard, and with it comes hard decisions. For so many of us, fear is what holds us back from deciding to do the things our hearts tell us to do. It's the fear of not getting it right. Hell, it's the fear of potentially *never* getting it right. Our logic tells us, "hell no" because of past failures.

These hard decisions are also the moments that will define us. Will we be resilient, or will we retreat into the shadows of our own doubts? This is one of the reasons why I wanted to write this book. There is a lot of weight in becoming a coach—let alone becoming an amazing coach. It took me years to take the leap, but when I did, I went all in.

That's the thing about taking the leap... once you fully commit, there is no looking back. It's like jumping out of a perfectly good plane.

Before I go any further, I have never jumped out of a plane. This is just my way of painting you a picture of commitment. I do believe this is a profound analogy, though, so stay with me. Where was I? Right, perfectly good plane.

Become an AMAZING Coach

You have had dreams of jumping out of a plane, because you want to feel the excitement and do something most people will never do. You sign up, take all the classes, and the next thing you know, you are standing at the door of the plane awaiting your epic experience. Then in the blink of an eye, you step out into the unknown. You never look back at the plane, because you know there is no going back. You have committed to this journey, and you know things will never be the same. You may free fall alone, but there are people waiting to guide you to the landing zone. You just need to trust them.

Not everyone has someone they can trust or someone to guide them, which is another reason I felt like it was important to write this book. There are a lot of people that never take the leap to become a coach because they don't know where to start, and they don't know where to start because they don't have anyone to help them. With this book I want to lend my knowledge and experience to anyone who is looking for guidance to just get started. There is so much information out there, and this is a great place to start.

With all beginnings there will be key subjects to consider. I could give you so many ideas and topics to choose from, but I addressed the areas that would have made the start of my coaching career so much easier. Though I don't regret anything I have gone through or learned, if I had to pick, these would be the areas that would have resulted in a smoother path for me to become an amazing coach. You will read about how I started coaching my first athlete, how having a mentor has given me a different perspective on how I coach, why the responsibility of being a coach is such a privilege, and how to overcome feeling like an impostor.

There are lots of coaches out there, so to set yourself apart, have a solid foundation of coaching values. The knowledge you will get from this book will set you up with the values of success and pave the way for you to touch many lives. You just need to see it in your future.

When you read this book, you will see your path become clearer, because you will have questions answered before they were even concerns. This doesn't mean everything will be clear in your coaching future. With any journey you can't look too far ahead, because you still need to be present to make decisions in the moment. Looking too far out will make things confusing if you have not yet decided on a solid plan. Set goals for the future, but make sure you stay grounded in your day-to-day progression.

Walk your path and keep this book close. When you need to check your coaching compass, you will have the tools that will help you be successful. Your success will ripple through your life and the lives of many others in the endurance community.

I talked about a couple of reasons I wrote this book, but I saved the best for last. The top priority for this book is to create a stronger endurance community. Bob Babbit told me in a conversation at Desert Tri in Palm Desert, CA, "To build a stronger community, we must all do our part." Since that conversation, that's what I have done. I believe that's what all of us must do. As a coach, I believe that it is my responsibility to help athletes keep the flame ignited within. That flame represents the reason they became an athlete in the first place. As coaches, we help fuel those flames—a privilege many will never understand. When we do it right, our community becomes stronger. That strength will inspire others to join, and that cycle is what will foster longevity in this sport and in all sports.

Prospective coach: You are needed, and this book is for you. Don't waste your gifts.

There is one person out there right now who is waiting for what you have to offer. Their journey can begin the moment you decide to become an AMAZING COACH!

1

THE **LIFE-CHANGING** START OF MY COACHING ADVENTURE

Who knew coaching could be
so rewarding?

I have always enjoyed the privilege of leading people. Throughout my Marine Corps career, I always did what needed to be done to be selected for leadership positions; I especially liked the position of managing the physical fitness of a unit. I remember the first time I was put in charge of the body composition platoon at Marine Corps Air Station Miramar, California. It was for overweight and/or out-of-shape Marines and Sailors. Being in charge of that platoon allowed me to make a large impact on a lot of people. I didn't know then what I know now (in terms of coaching), but it was so fulfilling to see members of that platoon make progress and lose weight—sometimes even 60 or 70 pounds. I had a lot of success in that position, so every year or every duty station I went to after that, I wanted to be involved in the physical fitness and preparation of others. Over time, this involvement in the betterment of others became a habit for me. It became a part of who I was and what I was known for amongst my peers.

In Albany, GA (after a deployment to Afghanistan), I suffered from severe lower back pain. I decided to start riding bikes as a way to stay fit without hurting my back, which led me to a local bike shop called Cycle World, owned by the Hoffman family—selfless people. The Hoffmans really reached out and allowed me to be a part of their cycling family. I remember the first day I went into Cycle World. They showed me a bike, but I wasn't really sure I wanted to commit yet. They told me to take the bike and try it out. If I liked it, we could discuss a final purchase, but if I didn't, no big deal! (Coming from California, I was NOT used to that kind of hospitality.) I took the bike—an aluminum GT with 105 components. It may have been old and heavy, but it did the job.

My first bike ride was with an older group of riders. I actually did pretty well (especially for a first ride), averaging around 19-20 mph on the 24-mile ride. I even got to experience my whole groin area going numb—something I hope to never relive again. I didn't know much about cycling etiquette or what the rules were at that time, so when it was my turn to get up front and pull (be the lead bike that everyone else could draft off), I just stayed up there leading the group for the last 5 miles, using as much energy as I had to keep the pace going. They didn't tell me until afterwards that I didn't have to stay up front that long, but they let me since it seemed like I wanted to do it. Lesson learned. Ha!

As a natural leader, I was thrilled when I was asked to substitute teach a spin class. My first class was great! Afterwards, I was asked by the owner to teach an hour-long class every Wednesday (after I got my certification from Mad Dog Inc.—the company that controls the spinning brand). This was the first time I'd ever taught anything in the civilian world, and it was totally different for me. I even had to pick a playlist! The first class had only one young lady who was there every Wednesday, but it grew to being completely packed within a year—if you didn't get to my class early, you didn't get in. From there, I got some personal training certifications and a nutrition certification through ISSA (International Sports Sciences Association). Soon after, I started teaching more group classes, and just generally helping people with their fitness goals. This was how I really got started as an endurance coach.

As I started approaching retirement from the Marine Corps, I started wondering what else I wanted to do with my life. I'm a paralegal, a Marine, a small weapons instructor, a martial arts instructor, and so much more. I made myself consider these questions: "What do I ENJOY doing?" Answer: Fitness. "What can I do that involves fitness, but also involves working with people?" Answer: Coaching! Plus, the Marines had taken me back to Southern California where I had a lot of opportunities to test the waters of the endurance coaching industry.

I started talking to people I had met in California that were coaching or being coached, and they provided me with the information I needed to eventually take on my first paid athletes. I was charging only about $35/month (if not just doing it for free) just so I could get my foot in the door and really learn what this coaching thing was all about. It has definitely evolved since then, because at first, I was just testing this out as a possibility for retirement. The coaching philosophy I have now did not exist back then. I was honestly just trying to make some money when I started. I was looking for people to pay me to tell them what to do—it was that simple. I found that I really enjoyed seeing people accomplish their goals.

It turns out, it wasn't really that simple. This is when I learned that if I only focused on the money, I would never make any money.

> " IF I **FOCUSED** ON THE PEOPLE, EVERYTHING ELSE WOULD HAPPEN THE **RIGHT** WAY. "

Two of my mentors (Jondi Bernardo & Brian Long) told me that if I focused on the people, everything else would happen the right way. While that resonated with me, I never dreamed I'd be able to touch as many lives as I have since the inception of my coaching business, Latitude Pure Coaching. It has been a great feeling to do something that I never thought I would be capable of doing. I never would have been able to fathom making a living doing something I enjoy so much. Most of the time when we think about getting paid or going to work, we think about doing things that we aren't exactly excited to do. I don't really believe that even people who claim to love what they do actually love what they do. I believe they love why they do it. My coaching why is helping people see that they are not alone in their journey. Some of the additional things I enjoy are the physical fitness development, the mentoring, and the relationships with

> "I AM ONE OF **MANY**
> GREAT EXAMPLES
> OF SOMEBODY WHO
> **NEVER** THOUGHT
> THEY COULD GET
> WHERE THEY **ARE**."

people—it all keeps me social, active, and happy. And when I feel like that, it's easier for me to pass these gifts on to other people.

I didn't think coaching was something I would ever be capable of. I didn't think I had enough intelligence, or enough smarts for people to trust me to help them achieve their goals. I was totally wrong. I am one of many great examples of somebody who never thought they could get where they are.

Coaching has brought so much joy into my life, and I don't know where I would be if I hadn't had the courage to try something different. Instead of looking back and saying, "I wish I would have…" or, "I probably could have…," I actually did it. Because of that leap of faith, my life is better, I am happier, and I can honestly say that I have impacted the lives of so many others. I can't imagine what my life would be without coaching.

2

THE REASON I KNOW YOU **SHOULD** BECOME A COACH

Easy. It's not all about you, remember?

Believe in Yourself

I am often asked why I became a coach. I always respond that coaching others is not just something I believe in—it's a passion. I sometimes even describe it as a superpower I didn't know I had. I think people just ask me this because they're trying to find a belief in themselves, but it's likely (if they already want to become a coach) they already have this superpower as well. While many people possess the power to impact or inspire others, only a few people will choose to use this power. It is for this reason why, for those few individuals, coaching is their calling. This is the reason why coaching is my calling. Although I am just one person, I can inspire many. Just one coach can ignite a flame in so many people. A single coach can truly impact hundreds of lives. As you read this chapter you will find the answer to the question that you have continuously asked yourself. Should I become a coach? Within this question lies your truth. Within this question lies your superpower if you choose to unlock it.

To unlock your superpower, you have to first believe in yourself. Self-belief is the power source for your superpower. It gives you the courage to take on challenges. It equips you with the drive to inspire others to do the same. Once you believe, you will be unstoppable.

Prospective coaches might doubt this superpower exists for them. Think of it like Keanu Reeves' character in The Matrix. He didn't believe he was The One, and he didn't want to believe that he had the power to do so much good for others. But over time, people encouraged him, they gave him knowledge, and they trained him to fulfill his destiny. Then the moment he started to believe? That's when everything changed for him. Believe in yourself. Believe that you can inspire somebody and change their life.

This belief in yourself is central to everything I'm going to share with you. I know it's hard to believe that you—just one person—can make a drastic change in someone else's life. I didn't believe it at the beginning, either! I had someone say to me early on, "When you get it, you're going to make so many people's lives different." But it took years for me to get it. It took a while for people to teach me, to mold me, and to believe in me more than I believed in myself before I got there. After seven or eight years now, I have finally started to believe it.

It's scary and different, but the moment you believe in yourself, you will unleash a power that will allow you to resonate on another level with everybody you meet. That power changes lives. That power helps people see their possibilities.

Impacting Lives

So let's talk about impacting people; helping others write their story. I think that **this** is the most valuable part of this book.

Everything about being a coach is about helping somebody else. You become the person that provides the pen. The conduit of possibilities. The guide. The person that your athletes look to for direction. Although their story has been going on for years (good chapters and bad), you can help them see that their story isn't over unless they decide to stop writing it. As a coach, you get to guide them on a journey that can be so profound that they might not even believe it. I've heard athletes say things like, "I can't believe my life has changed so much," or "I can't believe where I am now." You can help them continue to do great things.

One of my athletes was going through a lot of hard stuff in her life and she didn't believe in who she was. She didn't believe that it was possible for her to be more than she was at that time. She struggled with her self-confidence and her self-worth. She struggled with questions like, "Am I good enough to even be good enough for myself?" It's hard when you first meet athletes like this, athletes who are so deep in their own sorrow they can't see anything else. For me though, I've learned that this is when I need to shine the most. This is when I really need to show my athletes what they're capable of.

Over time, as this woman and I had conversations, as she did her workouts, and as she started to see the gains from all of our work together, what she was learning resonated past her training and into her life. I was showing her that she was enough, and that she had what it takes to be even more. Then everything changed. After I'd been coaching her for a couple of years, she said, "I don't know if I ever shared this with you, but you changed my life. You have helped me see myself and to take care of **me**. I was giving so much energy to other people's problems, that I didn't realize I was drowning in my own sorrow." That was profound to me. It was in that moment I knew that **this** was what I wanted to do as a coach—change lives. The first time you have a moment like this with one of your athletes, it will show you the value of becoming a coach.

Ripples

The impact of a coach doesn't stop with individual athletes, either. Think about being a coach as being that rock thrown into a pond that causes a million ripples. One action from a coach, one person helped, and the rippling effects can branch out through careers, families, and entire lives. The positive energy that you give them? That can be the hope they pass on to others. The resilience. The courage. All of those things that you help grow in your athletes can resonate throughout the world. Your positive influence will live, in this way, long after you're gone. I hope that these ripples really put into perspective how important being a coach can be, and how many lives you have the potential to touch.

This may all seem like a lot. You may be thinking, "There's no way that I could make that big of a change in somebody's life." But you can! You just have to choose to do it. You have to make the choice to follow your dream and be a coach.

> "YOU HAVE TO MAKE THE **CHOICE** TO FOLLOW YOUR **DREAM** AND BE A COACH.

You've already done more than most and taken the first step by reading this book. You clearly want more in your life. You want to make a change. You want to leave your mark. And you know what? You already have everything you need—you have that spark. My goal with this book is to give you the drive and the tools to become something that you never thought possible. You may not believe that you have the knowledge, or the time, or the experience, but you have the desire, and that's what matters. You have the feeling deep inside—the kind that you own. It's part of who you are. **That** is the reason you should become a coach.

Believe in yourself. Don't sell yourself short. Stop holding yourself back. Know better, do better, be better. You have everything it takes to impact so many lives—choose to use it.

3 WHY DO **YOU** THINK YOU SHOULD BECOME A COACH?

*Your purpose is what drives
you to AWESOMENESS.*

I n this book, I told you why I think you should become a coach. Have you asked yourself the same question? WHY should you become a coach?

The excitement of starting a potential new career can cloud your judgment. You have to become mindful of this. Try playing devil's advocate with your own thoughts. Be intentional—identify the places your knowledge base isn't as strong and anticipate the things that could come up or the things that could happen. You won't have all the answers in the beginning, nor will you be immune to some failure, but taking the time to evaluate your purpose upfront will benefit each future step on this journey.

I encourage you to dig deep for the answers to why you want to coach. If you have doubts, they should be addressed before you take on any athletes. The more intentional you are about your purpose, the greater your chance for success. The type of coach you are going to be depends heavily on the answers you find today. Ready? Let's begin.

Are you willing to be a counselor and a mentor?

Not many people are truly excited about taking on the hard times or struggles of others—it takes a very selfless individual to be open to this. I've seen people who are trying out coaching decide very quickly that it's not for them after they're confronted with an athlete's struggles on a personal level. I've talked to a number of coaches about this, and I've found that there are basically two responses. About half say something like, "I'm here to help them with their goals, not their problems." I wonder if they understand the connection between physical performance and mental or emotional health. (For example, when Tiger Woods was on top of the golf world, emotional drama in his personal life threw his focus out of whack, and he came plummeting down like a poorly stacked grocery display.)

The other half of the coaches say something like, "A good coach understands that they will have to be a counselor sometimes." These coaches get it—athletes are human beings, and they have all the emotions involved with being human. An amazing coach has to meet the athlete where they are mentally and emotionally each moment. Are you ready for that?

Why is helping people important to you?

I can remember the first time I asked myself why helping people was important to me. I was only able to come up with reasons why others help people. I could recall conversations, articles, and books I had read about others' journeys, but couldn't think of one time when I'd stopped to reflect on why it was important to ME. I wondered if others struggled with the answer as much as I did. I was actually so uncertain at that point that I wasn't able to answer this question until after a few years of coaching had passed. Or, should I say, after a few years of struggle had passed, because as I look back, nothing seemed to work or click for me until I WAS able to answer for myself why helping people was important.

But when it clicked, I knew. In an instant I knew my why, and everything changed. Things I previously struggled with became easy, and the inability to find quality athletes to coach became a thing of the past. Are you wondering what my answer was? I'll tell you this: it was something I never expected it to be.

> " I **NEVER** WANT ANYONE TO FEEL LIKE THERE IS NOT AT LEAST **ONE** PERSON ON THIS EARTH THAT **BELIEVES** IN THEM. "

Helping people is important to me because I never want anyone to feel like there is not at least one person on this earth that believes in them. I have since made it my purpose in life to be that one person to whomever asks for my help. Nothing great was ever accomplished alone, and it was then that I decided that nobody should ever have to try alone.

Being a coach is great, but are you being realistic?

It's so easy to say you want to do something when you're excited, before you really understand what the commitment will be. In the beginning of becoming a coach, it's like seeing a shiny object from 40-feet away. You get excited and start to walk toward the shiny attraction, and with each curious step the object becomes clearer. Finally, you get close enough to see what the object is, and your curiosity shifts to disappointment. It's not a diamond; it's just a piece of tinfoil. How do you prevent this disappointment in your coaching career? You go in with your eyes wide open. You begin coaching with an understanding that certain things you want to happen may or may not happen.

When I first started coaching, I believed that it would be a great idea to charge $300/month for my coaching services. I had done some research and I saw other coaches charging similar rates (with some charging even two or three times that amount!) I thought it would be easy. Hell, I was thinking I only needed one athlete and that would be the sign that I could always find another. I had just started coaching, nobody knew me, I hadn't coached enough people for word of mouth to be a thing, and I didn't have the experience needed to justify that fee. As you may have already guessed, I didn't get any new athletes. I didn't even get any inquiries! At the beginning I assumed a lot, and in turn, I was disappointed a lot. I have now learned that preparation will ready you for anything. Ask yourself in the beginning, "Is this realistic?" to minimize the number of let downs.

Are you able to put aside your needs for the welfare of your athlete?

I presented this question to a very good friend of mine and her feedback was, "This question scares me because it sounds super serious." I replied, "Coaching is some serious shit." With caution, she said, "It could possibly scare potential coaches away that just want to coach as a hobby."

Let me start with this: I am not saying you need to put yourself in harm's way or minimize your own day-to-day self-care.

I only want to point out that there will be sacrifices sometimes for the betterment of the athlete. There will be days when you're exhausted but an athlete will need your help. There will be days you'd rather spend with your family, but you are committed to coaching at a camp out of town. Life is, and will always be, full of sacrifices, but anything worth having will take real work.

A few years ago, I had an athlete that came back from a family vacation to find that her back door had been kicked in and she had been robbed. She had just paid me for the upcoming month of coaching, but once she told me what happened I felt I had a decision to make—send the money back and help her, or keep the money and use it to pay my own bills (she was not requesting a refund at all, mind you). I ended up doing what I felt was right. I sent the coaching fee back to her and told her the money could help her fix the door. I sacrificed my own income to make sure that my athlete, a member of my endurance family, knew that our relationship was deeper than money. I understand that we are all in different places and that we all have different needs, so each of these decisions will be highly personal, but how much we are willing to invest into our athletes will not only affect how they grow, it will determine how successful we become as coaches.

Are you in a place where you should be helping anyone other than yourself?

At any given time in our lives we are either going through something or we are on the tail end of getting over something. When we're looking for the right time to start a new chapter in our lives, we should ask ourselves this: Is there ever really a right time to start something new? That's the million-dollar question. The pessimistic view is that there is never a right time, so why bother? Or we could choose the path of optimism and believe that there is no better time than now. No time like the present. The truth actually lies somewhere in the middle, and only you can decide what is right. Do you spend time coaching athletes right now, despite so many other things going on in your world that need to be dealt with first? Or do you wait for your own life to settle down before taking on any additional responsibilities?

You are going to need to be more honest with yourself than you probably want to be, and you may have to make the hard decision of saying, "I'm not ready." This doesn't mean you can't coach in the future—it actually means that you are already choosing the best interest of your future athletes by delaying becoming a coach until you can provide your best to those athletes. It signifies your commitment to being the best coach you can be. It's decisions like these that are a true embodiment of what being an amazing coach is, and not everyone will take the time to consider these decisions or to contemplate what's right for others. Coaching will always be there, so don't let shame dictate your answer.

Are your intentions selfish or selfless?

There was a point in my own personal growth when I didn't really know the definitions of "selfish" or "selfless." Had I heard those words used before? Yes. But how many words have we all used (or heard others use) that we haven't looked up and read the true definitions for? If you know the definitions, just bear with me a moment... The Merriam-Webster dictionary defines SELFISH as, "lacking consideration for others; concerned chiefly with one's own personal profit or pleasure" and defines SELFLESS as, "concerned more with the needs and wishes of others than one's own; unselfish." I'd hope that if you're looking to become an amazing coach, you're looking to provide selfless service to your athletes. But I can't assume that just because you're reading this book, you're not selfish. I can only hope that if you have selfish tendencies but want to be a coach, this book inspires a change that helps you evolve into a coach/person that puts others' needs before their own (in a healthy way and not in a self-destructive way).

Selfish individuals have no place in the coaching world because no one can truly help others if they are only worried about themselves. If you are only looking to feed your own ego, or pad your own pockets, stop reading right now and find some other journey to embark upon—your kind is not welcome here. On the other hand, if you are all about helping people achieve what they previously deemed to be impossible, keep reading, because you are the kind of person we need becoming those amazing coaches.

> ## "NO ONE CAN TRULY **HELP** OTHERS IF THEY ARE ONLY WORRIED ABOUT **THEMSELVES**."

Your selfless commitment will bring a breath of fresh air to an athlete's journey.

Ask yourself these three questions: What is your coaching goal? How do you plan to meet that goal? Why do you feel (emotionally) this is important to you?

A lot of people confuse these questions—not only when it comes to coaching, but when it comes to life in general. Simon Sinek wrote a book titled, "Start with Why" which changed the way I coach and live. It helped me understand Why (the purpose), How (the process), and What (the product). These three concepts were fundamental to me becoming the coach I am today. Was it easy for me to answer these questions? No. Not at all. But the many hours I spent thinking about them was absolutely worth it, and here's why. I was confusing my Why and my What. Unfortunately, this happens for a lot of people.

For example, if I ask an athlete why they want to race a 140.6-mile triathlon, they usually tell me, "To become an Ironman." I explain to them that the title of Ironman is the What and not the Why. Their Why could be something like, "I want to set an example for my kids." This confusion is normal. After having hundreds of conversations with athletes over the years, I have learned that realizing the difference between Why and What is life-changing and brings people a new sense of purpose.

Keeping in mind that what you want to do is not the same as why you want to do it, you can find that deeper meaning—the Why of your desire to become a coach.

- **What is your goal as a coach?** Do you want to help athletes improve performance, do you want to help them improve their health, or something entirely different?
- **How do you plan to meet that goal?** Will you build a performance-based philosophy, or will you seek to just get people off the couch?
- **Why do you feel this is important to you?** Do you love the feeling that comes with showing someone they can perform at a higher level, do you want to help prevent heart disease because of a personal experience, or some other reason?

The people you coach will feel the energy you put into them. If your Why isn't solid, they will feel your hesitation and won't have an amazing experience with you. Don't rush through your answers, because you will need to come back to them time and time again when you need to be reminded of your Why. Losing your Why at any point will be a disaster for you as a coach and therefore a disaster for your athletes. An amazing coach would never let that happen.

———————

The ability to honestly look within is not a trait possessed by everyone, so give yourself credit for that. Remember, the foundation you lay at the beginning will be the support for the relationships you have with your athletes (and others) for years to come, so take the time to reflect on these questions up front—no matter how long it takes.

4

HOW CAN COACHING FIT INTO **YOUR** LIFE?

You still have time to take over the world.

wanted to start this section off by writing about something that I know happens to more people than probably any of us can fathom. It has definitely happened to me. We fill our schedules with chaos, but we often forget that this was all self-inflicted chaos. We put all sorts of things on our plates. We get these ideas (usually multiple ideas), and we add to our to-do lists, processes, structures, etc. We just add, and add, and add, and add to the plate until we get to the point where we don't have any idea how it happened, but we know that we have too much going on in our lives (forgetting that **we** took it all on). This is important as we talk about part-time coaching, because if you take this on, it's just another thing you're adding in to your life (something else to fill your plate). You may want to add part-time coaching to all of the other things you already have going on (career, family, social life, etc.) as a side hustle, or maybe as a hobby, or even just to have something that brings you a little bit of enjoyment. But when you put too much on your plate, it can be overwhelming—not just to you, but also to those around you.

When I started coaching part-time, I had a lot of trials and tribulations as I tried to find harmony within my schedule. It was a hectic time, and it put a lot of stress on me. The beginning of my endurance coaching career was also the beginning of my own endurance career as an age-group triathlete. There were a couple of big years in 2013 and 2014 when I took on a lot, including my first sprint triathlon, my first Olympic triathlon, my first 70.3, and my first Ironman. Also during this time, as a Marine, I was involved in the wars we were fighting and deployments to Afghanistan. I was newly married, and I had step-kids. I had so many responsibilities, and yet I still took on something else by deciding that I wanted to be a coach. Over time, this put a lot of stress on my career, my sanity (this was big), and my family (I went through a break-up during this time). I didn't really realize what I was doing or how much chaos I was causing in my own life, but it got to be too much to bear. I even got to the point where I needed professional help because my sanity was being challenged. I thought it was just anxiety because of things going on in my career, unhappiness I was feeling, or various other things happening in my life. What I figured out, though, was that I had simply put too much into circulation within my life, and I needed to take some things away. I had bitten off more than I could chew. As I came to terms with that, I was able to identify which things were too much, and which things were important. I was able to back off of some things and regain my own sanity.

There's no exact formula for how you can do this, but I believe that if I share the tips and tricks I've learned over the years, you can use them as tools to help alleviate some of this chaos for yourself. The whole idea of getting into coaching is to help people, but you can't help others if you're not able to help yourself.

Let's talk about what works.

1. Mindfulness

Mindfulness for me is being really present in the moment with what I'm doing, why I'm doing it, and making sure I SHOULD be doing it. I want to be aware, rather than let my life pass by. There are lots of times I still mess up. I still put too many things on my plate. But I'm more in tune with myself and I can now actually see the disruption in my schedule when this happens because I've developed mindfulness. To become more mindful, slow down, observe your thoughts, and question your actions.

2. Essentialism

I read a great book a while back called *Essentialism*, but it was just within the last year or two that I really started to understand the importance of it. Prioritize only what is essential. It taught me how to say a "comfortable no." It also taught me to learn how to focus on the things that really matter to me—to make sure that I wasn't doing something just because I thought I should. I learned to do only things that help me grow as a person, within my career, or within my family. Reading that book helped me eliminate doing too much.

3. Projects

Now I categorize my responsibilities into what I call "projects." I limit myself to only four projects. My four projects are my family, coaching, my training, and my personal growth. These are the four things I try to focus on every day. I've noticed that when I try to add too many other things outside of my project list, I start to feel my anxiety and stress levels go up. This affects my relationships with the other people in my life, including my athletes, and I don't want that to happen.

4. Fluid Focus

Another thing I do is to make it a point to put my family first, my training first, or my athletes first. You may be saying, "Don't you have to always put your family first?" or "How can you put that many different people **first**?" The answer: I focus on whoever I'm with. The less things you have on your plate, the easier it is to shift your focus. This is where that fluidity comes in—your focus can flow better when there is less to focus on. If I'm at home, I'm present at home. If

> "WHEN YOU SAY **YES** TO
> SOMETHING, THERE
> IS **LESS** OF YOU FOR
> SOMETHING ELSE. MAKE
> SURE YOUR **YES** IS WORTH
> THE **LESS**.
> -*LOUIE GIGLIO*

I'm training, I'm present with my training. If I'm speaking to an athlete, I'm present with them.

5. Presence

Before, there were so many things going on that I couldn't control any of them. I lacked the ability to be present. My mind wandered endlessly and I was always trying to do more or see further ahead into the future. This turned out to make my life overwhelming. That brought on headaches and restless nights of sleep. Then, in a moment, I realized I could only be effective when my mind wasn't going in a million different directions. So I quieted my mind (by reflecting on one single thought) and practiced using laser focus on the moment I was in. Learning to be more present, for me, has involved things like meditation, or by just learning how to be okay with being bored!

6. Be Bored

I've read some articles this year that talked about people not ever wanting to be bored. People are constantly busy. So I make it a point to just be bored sometimes. I let my mind be free, and I try not to focus on the TV or the telephone. I might just look out a window for a while—something that simple can help alleviate the stress in your life.

———————

To live your life and be a coach requires what most people would call *balance*. I, on the other hand, like to use the word *harmony* because I prefer things to be more fluid than flexible or balanced. With balance, there's a tipping point. Even when you think about flexibility, there's a breaking point. Fluidity, however, allows everything to move in harmony with everything else.

As I learned not to force myself to do all of the things I thought *needed* to be done, life became more enjoyable. My life became more consistent, and I now get joy out of all of the things I choose to do.

Consider what you have on your to-do list. That's important when trying to decide whether or not you want to add coaching into your life part-time. Is it on the list of things that are most important to you? If it is, and you are able to mindfully add it into your daily routine, you will be able to give your athletes the attention they deserve. Can coaching fit into your life with harmony?

This will all take a while. Nothing will happen for you overnight. But the thing you should consider first is how you're going to find harmony in your life when you start adding in extra things (like part-time coaching). Make sure that you're prepared to make those hard decisions like saying "no" to certain things because you want to say "yes" to others. Be able to honestly answer the questions, "Is coaching too much for me right now? Do I have the time to give to coaching so I can be as awesome as I want to be?"

A side bonus:

As you learn these things for yourself, and as you navigate this journey of growth, you will be even more equipped to help your athletes. You will also gain your own insight to share with them about how they too can eliminate some noise from their own lives, which will also help them be more consistent with training.

If you have too much going on in your life, you won't be able to be present for your athletes. You won't **be** an amazing coach if you don't **feel** amazing. This is also a very big part of your ability to see the need for growth in your athletes' lives. As you're seeing patterns in your own life that aren't working, and you have to decide what's important to you, you will start to see these patterns in your athletes as well. They're probably going through the same things you are. Just as you're growing, you'll see them grow as well. I learned not to take the important things in my life for granted, and the hard lessons I learned have taught me how to be successful, and how to incorporate harmony in my life. I'm passing these lessons on to you, just as I pass them on to my athletes every day.

Be aware, though, that even if an athlete **is** hitting all of their workouts, it doesn't mean that they don't have other areas to improve in—it doesn't mean that they have harmony throughout all the areas of their life. As you talk to them about this, and as you share your own journey and what worked for you, they will see you as an amazing coach. They will see that you care about more than just their fitness goals and their training—you care about how they feel and what is going on in their lives.

There are athletes that you will work with that will hit all their training milestones, but are still fighting an inner battle. Harmony is not always tangible. It's not just the choice between work or home life. It's not limited to choosing to train or spend time with the kids. In all athletes there has to be harmony in their emotions and thoughts, too. What is key to helping them is having the ability to be empathetic and compassionate. Then your athletes will know that you don't only care about them, but that you are invested in them. When you do this, the athlete's growth and happiness will be immeasurable.

———————————

Your journey of self-growth will teach you that you can be a part-time coach and also a husband, a wife, a sister, an employee, or whatever else is important to you. You can be awesome at more than one thing—you just have to make intentional choices about what those things will be. Avoid over-filling your plate. Find how coaching can fit into your harmony.

5

NOT **EVERYONE** WANTS TO PUT IN THE EARLY WORK

The decisions in the beginning will dictate your success.

Most people, when thinking about starting a new job or a new career, underestimate how much time and energy it will actually take to make it happen full-time. It's also worth taking a look back at the career they've been in up until that point, because after anyone has been in something for maybe ten to fifteen years (or more), it's likely that a certain level of complacency has been developed. It's easy to forget how we got where we are, and that can give us the misconception that we can jump directly into the intermediate or advanced level in a new career or new passion. That, however, is not the case.

I started coaching maybe fourteen or fifteen years into my Marine Corps career. I saw all of these other coaches and what they were doing. I wanted that life, but I didn't take the time to actually stop and think about the fact that they'd probably been coaching for a while. I didn't understand at that point that I should have been looking at the work that got them there, and not what they were doing at that moment. When you see people where they are right now, you usually don't see the foundation they had to lay years ago to get to this point. You see the results of their hard work, but not the struggles it took to get there.

If I could give you anything, it would be this: Don't look at where people are right now; look at where they started. Talk to them. Ask them questions about what they have been through. What you learn can be very vital to your development as a coach.

Lay down the foundation you want to build upon. You have all the time in the world to build your business, but you only have right now to create a solid start. You have laid many foundations in your life from completing kindergarten to your first credit card. Think of the knowledge you would be missing if you hadn't laid the foundations in these areas. To start, you can learn how being organized, creating structure, and understanding your finances will lay the foundation for a successful coaching business.

Many people are moving so fast that they can't even see what they're doing. We can get so excited about doing something different, or we get so spun up and motivated to make something new happen, that we overlook the small details. That can make our lives really, really hard. The key to a successful transition into a new career (or anything new) is to learn how to slow ourselves down and pay attention to the details. You've probably heard the saying, "The devil's in the details"? That's because those small details, when not respected, can be the devil. They can wreak a lot of havoc on your life and your sanity.

There are three critical steps that must be taken to have a successful coaching business. I didn't know what I didn't know when I started, but now I do (and I'm going to tell you). Keep reading to make less mistakes than I did.

1. Organize

Think of the easiest way to organize what you're doing that gives you a direction for where you want to go. If you try to just shotgun blast all of your ideas at once, you're going to end up working harder than you need to. The key is that you want to work smarter, not harder. The way to do that is to be more organized; but being organized looks different to everybody. My preference is bullet point lists—I like having questions that inspire me to think about things. Other people like to write down notes or keep a legitimate journal. You can use a Word document, or keep lists on your phone. Just get your thoughts down however you need to. The bottom line is that these organizational skills are going to be very vital as you progress, because there will be a lot of moving parts that you are going to have to consider. You have to have a well-structured platform for your business to be successful.

Starting out, for example, you might have a list like this:

- How will I invoice my athletes?
- How will I write training plans?
- How will I organize my taxes?
- How will I organize my outgoing & incoming expenses?

Here's a more specific example. I know I'm going to do taxes, so I'll make a list with bullet points (see below) and then I'll build from there.

Taxes

- Who is doing my bookkeeping?
- What is the filing deadline?
- What expenses can I write off?
- How much will it cost me to do my taxes?

There are so many different ways to organize, and so many pieces to organize when you're first starting out. The key is to just get it out—don't be so worried about what it looks like the first time. Organize from beginning to end; from basic processes to how you'll bring on a new athlete. Just get your thoughts on a piece of paper, and then step back from it. Come back to it later and look at it again, or even have someone else look at it. It can be helpful to have a friend or mentor look over your plan or your processes and see if they have input on how you could better structure things. They might even see things you're leaving out. You will have less stress over time if you think things through in the beginning. Don't spend more time than necessary on something that won't even really matter in the long run.

2. Structure

Think about whether you want to work for yourself or work within a group/company. Working for yourself is the first possibility. It's a harder way to go, but it can be a "risk is worth the reward" type thing. For me, I was always seeing these other coaching companies with their own gear and their own athletes, and I wanted that. I wanted my own team. I wanted to be able to bring my gifts to the table and share them on my own terms. And it is so rewarding and so fulfilling on a daily basis to look out and see a picture of my team or see an athlete at a finish line with team gear on and think, *I did that. I created that*. I always ask my athletes for their input, but basically, I make it happen.

Working for yourself is such a very empowering place to be, because we are usually living our lives under the direction of so many other people that it's nice to do things under our own vision. We can also then see (and benefit from) the fruits of our own labor. The amount of work you put into this is what you get out of it. So really, I would say the possibilities are endless.

Working for yourself gives you:

- complete responsibility over the business (along with complete reward)
- the ability to be at the ground level; to see what the athletes really want
- the freedom to make creative decisions
- the freedom to spend your revenue the way you see fit (on things **you** feel would bring your athletes value)
- the ability to create a business around the type of athlete that really resonates with you

To me, it's just like painting a picture, or building a motorcycle, or re-building the engine in a car. It's that creative feeling that you get. The feeling of, "I did this. I made this from nothing." You get to know that you laid the foundation for something that, in the end, can have endless possibilities with regards to the lives it can touch. This, to me, is the biggest selling point of running your own full-time coaching business.

Now let's talk about working for somebody else. If you want to do this, you can find a group of coaches that work under the same philosophy you do. The benefit of this is that as long as you're making enough money to support your lifestyle, you can do this without worrying about the bills, or worrying about the taxes, or worrying about the creative designs or the marketing. Somebody else can worry about that and you can just focus on your coaching! You can be more free to do what you do best—help others. If you're getting into coaching to have fun, this might be your route—letting someone else handle the business and administrative side of things. Because guess what? Business isn't always fun, but it's always necessary.

Working for someone else is sometimes a first step towards working for yourself. You can learn how to coach and learn how to run a coaching business from someone who's invested in your success.

3. Finances

The third thing to consider is also the biggest. It's very important. I get amped up when I think about this part because if you don't take it seriously, you will go broke. Will you be a part-time coach, or a full-time coach? If you go broke as a full-time coach, you won't be full-time coaching anymore. When you're coaching part-time, you still have something to fall back on. You probably still have a main source of income, and if the part-time thing doesn't work out, it's ok.

When you're full-time, however, it's all or nothing—you're either all in or you're broke. This is the part that can make full-time coaching scary.

This one really hits home for me. As I come to a point in my career when I'm transitioning into full-time coaching (even though people already think I'm full-time), it's a scary thing. It's an endeavor that has to be taken on very seriously. You have to do the math to determine if it is a viable option, and some people lack the ability (or the drive) to do this. If you're not structured and organized, you're going to miss a lot of pieces. Think about this: You set your coaching budget, but you forgot to account for something. Now you're losing $300/month, and that's huge! That's income out of your pocket. Or think about this: You forgot to account for taxes (that you now have to pay yourself) and you might be thinking, "Yes! I'm making $60,000/year!" But if you didn't remember to take taxes out, you're not going to be that happy when taxes are due. The bottom line is that unless you have a very detailed understanding of (and structure for) the financial responsibility piece of all of this, you might end up full-time coaching for part-time money. I give it maybe four to six months before you decide, "This ain't working."

Have you ever heard of business owners who are continually taking money out of their own register? Not having a good structure upfront is like that. If you can't account for all of your funds correctly, there's no way you can sustain a business. And if you can't sustain your business, how can you sustain your lifestyle? It's all up to you—if you don't make money, you can't eat. If you make money, you can eat (and maybe feed somebody else!) If money and math/accounting are not your strong suit, you either want to learn fast, or find somebody who can help you. Financial instability is one of the biggest downfalls of most companies. You have to understand every dollar you spend and every quarter you give, because over time, that money adds up and could have been hundreds of dollars that could have paid the bills or put food on your family's table. Don't take the financial side of this lightly. Sit down and make a very strict budget—don't assume the business is going to make a lot of money. Account for **every** dollar you spend, as well as the money you're bringing in. This will give you a better picture of how much money you're actually making.

It's important to know how very serious this financial stuff is. One year I made $75,000 just from coaching, but after all expenses (including paying taxes) I only took home $24,000 in actual income. That's a giant difference! Things add up really quickly. My advice is, right now, take a look back through your receipts or credit/debit card statements for the last 30 days. Add up every little transaction you made. "Man! I spent $600 on what?!" Did you say something like that? People don't usually pay attention to where all of their money is going, and then it's gone and they don't know where it went. But when it's your business, you have to be in the weeds with this stuff. Almost anybody can coach, but not everybody can run their own business. And going full-time? That's your own business.

> **MONEY** IS A BIG DEAL. **MONEY** IS A BIG DEAL BECAUSE OUR **LIVES** ARE A BIG DEAL.

Money is a big deal. Money is a big deal because our lives are a big deal.

Getting started in coaching takes some work. You've got to be willing to put in the time and effort to get the details sorted out. As you have read, full-time coaching comes with important steps that have to be taken. There are coaches that will not take any of these steps and you will see them pass through coaching like a season. For a crop to grow you must invest the time. Because everybody wants some of the fruit, but not everybody wants to bother planting the seeds or watering the crops. That's real.

Become an AMAZING Coach

6
START WITH THE FRIEND THAT BELIEVES IN YOU

Ask Mikey- he will for sure do it.

Your First Athlete

Let me give you a little story about me... I met a guy when I was first getting into endurance sports—when I was in the midst of training myself. I didn't know a lot, and I had some people helping me. I was also doing some of my own research, talking to other athletes, and reading some books on all of this. So, during this time, I met this guy, Justin. He is a really great friend of mine now. Justin hadn't done a triathlon yet. He was in the Navy. He was a great Sailor and a great family man, and was just looking for something else. At that time we were in Oceanside, CA, which has a great endurance community, and we really got bit with the triathlon bug. So I told him, "Hey man. I'll coach you for your first event." I think the first event he did was a duathlon, and I was able to give him tips on swimming and running. I think I was also sending him workouts through e-mail. (If I remember correctly, I ended up coaching his wife for her first 70.3 as well.)

Coaching your first athlete is something that intimidates most people when they're starting out. (Remember, I've been there.) You're probably asking yourself, "Who would I coach? Who would allow **me** to coach them?" Don't look too far though. Sometimes the best people to coach are your friends! You don't have to get to know them, and you don't have to figure out who they are. You don't have to wonder if they'll allow you to try things with them or if they'll be there for you. Those relationships are already tested and tried and you already know their true personalities. Your crazier friends will probably jump right in, while your more reserved friends might want to know more about what you're thinking—either way, this is a good place to start. Honestly, you probably already have friends that have been watching you train and race and may want to reach out to you anyway. Maybe they caught the bug or are ready to move forward on their journey, and guess who they have been thinking about calling? You! The person they already trust and know.

"A true friend supports you because they want to see you succeed." No matter what, the true friend is always looking for the best for you. That's what it comes down to.

"A TRUE FRIEND **SUPPORTS** YOU BECAUSE THEY WANT TO SEE YOU SUCCEED." A TRUE **FRIEND** IS ALWAYS LOOKING FOR THE BEST FOR YOU.

Caring About The Person

I've coached friends, I've coached my own kids, and I've even coached my best friend before. I've found that when you already love/care about somebody and you already believe in them, you do a lot of intentional work on your own growth because you want to be the best for them. When you know that they are putting a large amount of responsibility in your hands, you go read, you go ask questions, you go research, you reflect, and you're generally more intentional about how you approach coaching them. It's like being in any good relationship. "I don't want to mess this up, so what do I need to know to make it work?" "What tools will I need to be successful moving forward?" That's what you do when someone is that close to you, so take advantage of that by first coaching a friend.

The way you treat the person closest to you is the mold you should use for how you treat every athlete that you meet—I think this is why my coaching is successful. How would you treat somebody you love? You would go out of your way, show them that you are there for them, and you'd be honest with them. If you take that approach and use it with every athlete, you will bring value to the relationships that you create—especially with your future clients.

Sharing Success

Another thing that really felt great for me as I was coaching my friend Justin was the first time that he accomplished a goal. I just got that *wow* feeling. You may not technically consider yourself a coach yet, but if you help somebody achieve a goal, you coached them. You were there. You were sharing in their accomplishment. That's leadership. That means you have ownership over their successes, and even their losses. Never feel embarrassed about having tears of joy for your athlete's success. It's a good thing for you to be emotional around this process— it means you're invested. When you should really question yourself is if you have no feeling either way. If you feel, "it is what it is," then maybe coaching isn't for you. If you feel that way, I'd guess you probably don't possess what it takes to really show your athlete that you are there for **them** and not just a paycheck. So every time they accomplish something, celebrate it with them. Embrace that feeling. Even though Justin did the race, I was on the journey with him the whole time. I enjoyed it so much that it made me want to go on that same journey with other people just to watch them grow and accomplish their goals. You can't put a price on that. And you know what? If I had never started coaching, I never would have experienced this feeling. I think about how if I'd never started coaching, I would never have gotten to see Justin, my friend, change his life, or that change lead to a change for his wife, and then possibly his children down the line.

I think about that web of events in life that happens to lead people in different directions. It's like the movie *Final Destination*. One thing affects another, that affects another, and so on. I decided to try coaching and Justin saw me in that arena and said, "I trust you. Will you help me?" I said I'd help him and then we both learned something. We met other people. And then his wife saw him doing it, and she did something different and amazing. And now we're all affecting countless other people's lives. Now that they've moved forward with their family, they have stories to tell their children. It's going to affect so many people over and over again, and that's what it's all about.

Learning with Someone You Already Trust

I learned so many things through that first coaching process with Justin—how to communicate with people, how to build training sessions, and how to deliver training plans. I made sure that I learned a whole lot because I wanted to do right by Justin. I wanted to do what I needed to do so that I could give him the skills and techniques he needed to be successful. And because we were friends, he also gave me a lot of good feedback and asked a lot of good questions. (He actually asked a **lot** of questions...) So throughout this process, Justin and I got to grow together. He grew as an athlete, I grew as a coach, and our friendship grew. Coaching Justin was a great experience.

Getting feedback from Justin forced me to learn so much more, and it was a really good experience to be able to give something back to somebody that I cared about. Overall, you're more likely to get honest feedback from somebody you're close to. They can tell you things that others can't (or maybe wouldn't feel comfortable telling you). They will know how to deliver the information in a way that leaves you open to hear it. The feedback might be harder to hear, but when it comes from someone you care about, it's easier to learn and grow.

Friends and family have already opened up with you and been vulnerable with you about other subjects, so they're more likely to open up with you about their training, what they're going through, and how they feel. When an athlete feels comfortable telling you their personal struggles, you will see how those struggles affect their performance. This is like finding gold for a coach, because now you will be able to understand what is holding them back, and being that type of coach will unlock the true potential in athletes. All of this makes you a more experienced coach. When you actually get athletes that are vulnerable with you and that want to let you know what's going on with them, it teaches you about different people, but it also teaches you a lot about yourself. If I had a penny for every time I realized something about myself from something personal that an athlete shared with me, I'd probably be a rich man. That's where being open to hearing different perspectives and learning new things is really going to help you.

It still amazes me that even though there was so much I didn't know when I first started coaching Justin, I was still able to change his life because I wanted to know more. If I can repeat that life change every day with my athletes, then I can say I'm actually making a difference in somebody's world.

Who Will You Coach?

I think that what I went through is the kind of example that I want to give to any of you who are really on the fence about coaching or about who you need to coach first. It's not easy helping somebody out, and that's why finding the right person to get started with is going to really determine how far you go (and the kind of experience you have) within the coaching realm.

When you say, "Ok. I need to find this one person, but I don't know anything. I don't feel like I have enough experience to help them," just remember: it's not about having a whole lot of experience. The key is for you to understand what level you're on, and what level of athlete you need to connect with first. When you're a beginning coach, don't go out and try to get a pro-level athlete. You don't know enough yet. You don't have enough technical skill, know-how, or experience to help them be their best. If you're just starting off, start off with people who are just starting out in the sport.

A friend, James, once told me, "All you have to know is just a little bit more than the person that you're helping." It's with that you will find growth. And as you grow in your experiences, you go from helping just your friend or just that one individual to helping two or three friends. The word will spread, and at some point, you will look back and think, "Man. I remember when..." So don't look down on yourself before you even give yourself the ability to try. Don't say where you can't go before you even try to get to the starting line. It's a big step, but it's worth it. I look back and think that it's crazy... I coached Justin on some of his first events, and since then he has had a family and done ultramarathons and I've built a coaching business and coached many more athletes. You never know how you will affect somebody, the growth that you will inspire in them, or the adventures that you will encourage. You will show them that they have the ability to do so much more than they thought they could, and you will learn the same about yourself.

There are going to be many times in your life when you have to "just get started." You have to start with just one person. Just that one friend in your corner, and with just one belief that something really big can happen if you do this right. Coaching the people close to you will bring you that much more joy and excitement as you're starting this journey. You can branch off from there, and the possibilities are endless at that point.

So the question I have now is, who will you coach?

7
DON'T BE **INTIMIDATED** BY WHAT YOU DON'T KNOW

The impostor must be dealt with immediately.

Impostor Syndrome

There are a lot of pieces in this book that I believe can significantly help you begin to form a tangible idea of the direction you want to go. These pieces, if you let them, can also influence how good you will be when you get there—wherever *there* is for you.

When I talk to people who are contemplating coaching, their responses usually tell me that the biggest thing that intimidates them is a fear of what they don't know. They don't know if they have enough experience. They don't know if they can do it without a certification. They don't know if they know enough to **get** the certification. They don't know, and they don't feel like *enough*. They just don't know if they are ready. The truth is, though, that nobody is ever ready. At some point, you just have to get ready. You have to start the journey somewhere in order to have room to grow. I truly believe that what is happening with most people at this point in their journey is that they are fighting the feeling of being an impostor. That's the bottom line.

I asked another coach I know a question about this out-of-place feeling. I asked him, "What is one thing you wish you knew at the beginning of your coaching career?" He said he wished he could go back to the beginning and erase the feeling of being an impostor. He realizes now that this was just fear, and he can see how it held him back.

To me it is self-doubt, lack of confidence, and uncertainty all wrapping you up like a hot dog in a little croissant (pig in a blanket). At times it makes you feel scared and alone, because you distance yourself from others so they can't see your imperfections. It's the Bogeyman under your bed, and you're afraid to check if he really is there. That's what the impostor syndrome is. It's fear. It's the fear that if you don't know everything you think you should, somebody is going to see you for who you really are—a fraud. As I see it, though, you can only be an impostor if you're coaching for the wrong reasons.

> IF YOU'RE IN IT TO **HELP** OTHERS, IF YOU'RE TRYING TO **GROW** YOURSELF AND YOUR ATHLETES, AND IF YOU'RE ACTIVELY **SEEKING** OUT INFORMATION, YOU'RE NOT AN IMPOSTOR.

If you're in it to help others, if you're trying to grow yourself and your athletes, and if you're actively seeking out information to answer the questions you don't know, you're not an impostor. You're just a person at the beginning of their journey, and that's okay.

I have certainly felt that way, and I would venture to guess that all coaches have.

Honestly, if you feel like an impostor, it might just be a positive sign that you want to do better. You want to grow. You want to learn the things you don't know. You want to be better for your athletes. Use this feeling as a motivating factor to further yourself. No coach has all of the answers at the beginning. We all have to start somewhere, and earnestly following your journey from the beginning will make you even better at helping your athletes do the same.

Always Be Willing to Learn

You're not going to know it all. As a matter of fact, there will be a **lot** you likely don't know—how to build a plan, how to deal with multiple athletes, or how to answer every possible question that is going to get thrown at you. You know what? That's ok. Just be willing to learn. Spend the time educating yourself. Be ok with saying, "I don't know" and follow it up with, "but I will find out and get back to you." This combination of humility and willingness to do the work is what will make you an amazing coach. This time that you put in will assuage your fears and it will quiet your inner voice that's screaming, "Impostor!" You will become stronger and wiser, and eventually **you** will be the person passing this information on to a new coach as they start their own journey.

Don't sell yourself, or your journey, short because you are fearful of the unknown. Cut out the negative self-talk. It's natural to want to be the best at everything you do, but you don't have to be *the best*. You just have to be willing to do **your** best. If you can be honest with yourself about where you are and how hard you're willing to work to improve every day, you're already way ahead of some of the people who have been doing this for twenty or thirty years.

Never be complacent. Be intentional about improving your skills and your craft and it won't matter who you deal with—you'll be able to bring them some value, even if just a little bit. Be humble enough to say, "I am starting from nothing, but I want to become something." This is the key to your success. I know coaches who have been doing this for a long time that still learn from their athletes. They still grow and make changes. You will never be an impostor if your heart is in the right place.

"A JOURNEY OF A THOUSAND **MILES** BEGINS WITH A SINGLE **STEP**.
-*CHINESE PROVERB*"

8

THE SEARCH FOR YOUR JEDI **MASTER**

*On a great journey you
should seek out a guide.*

When you are on any new journey, it's always good to have a guide. The excitement of a new journey and the desire to learn everything and do everything all at once can sometimes impair your judgment or your willingness to ask for help, and having a guide will help with these things.

There are so many stories I could tell you about times when I insisted on doing something on my own that could have been **so** much easier if I had just asked somebody for help. Remember, though, that going through the learning period is usually the best way to learn how to do things well. We learn by doing and by repetition. Plus, knowing what **not** to do is just as important as knowing what you should do.

I want you to be excited about this initial stage of your coaching career. The successes **and** the times of adversity are all important experiences for you to be able to back up your coaching philosophy and your advice to athletes. Through it all, your guide will be there to be a sounding board, to share their experiences, and generally to support you as you grow as a coach. Also as you embark on this epic journey, don't get discouraged if you don't find your guide in the first few go-arounds. Try and try again, until you are successful in locating the right guide/mentor for you.

Don't Be Afraid to Reach Out

When I first started coaching, I asked a lot of questions. I was always seeking information from a lot of different people like Jim Vance, Chuck Kemeny, Jondi Bernardo, and Tom Fitch. Between talking to these other coaches and the books I read (which wasn't nearly as much as I read now), I was always trying to figure out how others were doing it; how they were making it happen. The people I reached out to were always willing to talk.

Unfortunately, most people don't even think about reaching out to other coaches when they are starting out! You might be thinking that you are so low on the totem pole in the coaching world that these other, more experienced coaches, might not take the time to talk to you or to help guide you. Or you might think that a veteran coach or a well-known coach has too high of a standing and would be very guarded with their information or maybe that they would just never talk to **you**. You never know until you ask! If they do take the time (and they probably will), you can learn so much from the knowledge they have to share, and you'll have the opportunity to learn from the experiences they have already been through—including their mistakes.

Paying for Guidance

You could also consider paying someone to mentor you. It's just like paying for a college course—you're paying a fee so that someone will share their knowledge with you. A long time ago, I was thinking about paying a certain coach to ghost coach me (shadow me while I was coaching athletes and give me his feedback), but a close friend of mine gave me some invaluable advice. He asked if I knew that coach already or if I'd ever even talked to him before. I said, "No, but he seems like a good coach!" My friend said that he'd been watching this coach for quite a while, and didn't think it would be worth the amount of money he wanted to charge me ($500/month). I was reminded that just because someone charges you a lot of money doesn't mean they'll be a good fit.

> "JUST BECAUSE SOMEONE **CHARGES** YOU A LOT OF MONEY DOESN'T MEAN THEY'LL BE A **GOOD** FIT."

He suggested I look around at other coaches who would actually help me grow, and would probably charge half that amount (if not do it for free). A light bulb went off for me. That made so much sense—why hadn't I thought of that? My friend told me about a few coaches he knew, and I went on a search for somebody to help me (I never did hire someone, but I know it would have helped).

Become the Athlete

Mostly I learned how to coach by hiring people to coach me. I would hire somebody to coach me for a specific event and then I'd watch how they did things. I'd learn from them. During my time as an athlete I've had about nine different coaches. I learned something from all of them—technical skills, different ways of writing workout structures, communication styles, or even random things that I decided I'd never bring forward or do with any of my athletes. All of these coaches were mentoring me while they were coaching me and I didn't even realize it at the time.

As I got wiser about the coaching world, I learned how to really vet the people that I learned from. I wanted to know what level of coaching they were at, what their expertise was, and about their coaching philosophy. Then I ran into the coach I have now, Chuck. He continues, to this day, to teach me something on a daily basis. We talk about all different kinds of things—business/financial aspects of coaching, athlete interactions, building workouts and training plans, etc. He gives me input on all of these things by being my coach, but also by being somebody I can bounce ideas off of. He is my mentor coach—he is my guide.

Trust the Process

I know it won't be easy for everyone to just go out and find a mentor—it's a process. You have to be patient about it, and you have to be willing to keep your eyes and ears open for someone who really reflects the direction you want to go in. That's what Chuck was for me—a reflection of the kind of coach I wanted to be. And now it's actually gotten to the point where we respect each other enough as coaches that he asks **me** questions! I remember one of the first times he wanted my opinion on something—it was so profound. I was shocked, and I said something like, "You want my opinion? Shouldn't that shit be the other way around?" He told me that he doesn't know everything, and that even he has the ability to continue learning. That's how I knew I was with the right person. I just knew it.

Once you decide you want to be a coach, my advice is to go out there and find your Jedi Master. Find somebody that you respect and believe in. Find someone who is willing to teach you the fitness and science aspects, but also the ways of coaching, the way to work with people, etc. Maybe spend some time as their athlete first and see how they do things. See how their style of coaching resonates with you.

Then try a different coach—one that is totally different than you so you can see the other side of the spectrum. Try things different ways and let others force you to think outside of the box—to step back and look at things through a different lens. Don't just run out and get a mentor and then find out down the line, once you get to know them, that they are not at all the right fit for you. Spend time being coached by various people, get the experience you need, and you just might find your mentor in the process.

You Never Outgrow a Mentor

Chuck continues to bring a new light to me as both an athlete and a coach, and I know my relationship with him is still a very integral part of who I am as a coach. Having a mentor coach throughout your career, and not just at the beginning, is important. Like Chuck said, everybody has the ability to continue learning. You just have to have an open enough mind to hear different points of view, even if you never agree with them. You'll get little pieces of information from what you hear that will inspire you to form new ideas that you can use to help somebody else.

The bottom line is that having a mentor coach is very important for your growth and can determine how successful you will be with your own athletes. It is not something that will happen immediately, but it is worth the time to find the right mentor.

9
THE **BAD** AND THE **UGLY** ABOUT COACHING

It's not all unicorns and rainbows. It's also dark and cloudy sometimes.

When telling someone that they should try something new, to make it sound more appealing, we often leave out the bad and the ugly. I know you understand what I'm talking about. It's like having those friends that are always trying to get you to try a pyramid scheme... They tell you how these one or two individuals got rich with the program, but never share what you have to go through to get there. (Not to mention that said friend is broke!)

I'm not going to do that in this book. I'm going to share all of the information that I feel will help you get started coaching. Your preparation is fundamental to your success, so let's venture into some of the subjects that caused me some difficulty when developing my coaching business.

Ugly Truth 1: Not Everyone Gets It

When I first started coaching, I thought everyone wanted to hire a coach. The naïve part of my brain also thought that everyone knew what a coach did. Years later I've learned that some athletes often have no clue what they want or need. There are so many factors around why people decide whether or not to hire a coach. The top three that stand out for me are finances, (perceived) athletic ability, and the athlete's knowledge of the sport. Additionally some athletes just don't understand coaching. Athletes view coaching as a product that is a simple transaction of "I pay you to tell me what to do." They don't understand that coaching is the partnership of a student and a teacher. Without this understanding, athletes often just pick a coach with the best deal. I wish I would have known this a long time ago. I would have saved myself from the belief that no athlete would ever hire me.

Some athletes just don't value coaching as much as others. There are athletes out there that believe they have it all figured out. I don't believe this to be true, though, because we all have room to grow. I used to try to get people to understand why they needed a coach by preaching about it until I was blue in the face. Then I realized that it's like the old saying, "You can lead a horse to water, but you can't make him drink." Since then I have had the realization that I should merely voice my opinion and then allow the athlete to do what they will with the information.

You also have athletes that just don't know what a coach does. It's bad for business when they don't know, but it's a great opportunity for you to teach them the value of having a coach. Point being, the athletes don't know what they don't know.

Athletes don't hire who they don't know (or at least who their training buddies don't know). Like the G.I. Joe cartoon says, "Knowing is half the battle." (Wow, am I really that old?) Be willing to learn about each potential athlete, and as you take the time to learn about them, the athletes can also get to know you. Plus, the more you can understand about how each athlete thinks, the more effective you will become as a coach.

I am pretty sure that at some point in your life you've come across someone that didn't seem to understand the hard work you had to put in to get something accomplished. I know sometimes this frustrates me, and I can only assume that I am not the only one that feels this way. One thing I have learned from this is that it's ok that athletes don't understand. Why? Because they hired a coach *because* they didn't understand. The sooner you accept this, the less it will frustrate you. Yes. I said "less" because no one is perfect, and there will be many times your ability to be patient will be tested.

Ugly Truth 2: When Coaching Gets Consuming

Let's talk about boundaries. Whether you have one athlete or twenty-five athletes, you better set the precedent from the beginning when it comes to boundaries. In the beginning, I wanted to be there for my athletes no matter what, but I didn't see that I was setting myself up for hardship in the future. This was challenging for me. One of the reasons I love coaching is because I get to interact with so many different people. Oh, but did I learn the hard way...

Not defining the boundaries upfront started to cause large amounts of stress in my family life—and that is only one area that it can affect. It can also negatively affect your career, your mental health, and your physical health. This stress can really kill your coaching motivation. I have even heard of coaches dropping coaching altogether to rebuild their lives—basically, they have to do a hard reset to get back to their happy place. Think about where they would have been if instead, they'd understood boundaries in the beginning.

What are boundaries? In my own words, boundaries keep us from going too far or overdoing something. As stated before, in my case my lack of boundaries hurt my family. I wasn't keeping coaching out of dedicated family events—I was still texting and answering athlete calls. This is no longer an issue, but I have to be very mindful of never letting this happen again. Though you may be very zealous about coaching, it should never destroy your life. When you are coaching, focus on coaching. When you aren't coaching, focus on what is in front of you. Boundaries will keep your life and your athletes' lives safe and full of happiness. This may be something that some athletes won't understand, but it is an important piece of the puzzle for their success—and yours.

Ugly Truth 3: There is a lot of Communication Involved

On many occasions, one of my new athletes (that has been with me less than 30 days) wants to move a training day or (the most common request) they want to combine days. Both of these things are doable, but it should only be done after the athlete has communicated with me first.

Here is why—the athlete doesn't always understand the intent of the workout structure. You may have even explained it to them, but that doesn't mean they fully understood. Or the athlete may have been self-coaching before working with you, so this means they have been used to doing a lot on their own. Either way, when they hired you as a coach, they didn't know what to expect, so you have to be patient enough to teach them your process. You may have to explain it again, and sometimes they still don't really understand. The truth is that they don't know the time or energy that goes into building their plan, and we as coaches need to be aware of this from the start.

The more we communicate with our athletes, the more we will have time to teach them. Don't get frustrated. Spend that energy helping them understand. This process starts the very first time you speak to the athlete. It is then when you will need to articulate what you do and how you do it. This will also help the athlete understand your worth as a coach. Because when an athlete doesn't understand what you do, it gets harder to justify them paying you what you believe your services are worth. Which brings me to the next ugly truth.

Ugly Truth 4: Setting Your Pricing is a Big Deal

How do you determine what to charge athletes that want to hire you? This question alone may be one of the most asked questions by new coaches, and it may also be the hardest one to answer. Sometimes I wish I was rich just to avoid dealing with charging athletes altogether. I'm telling you— no amount of research will prepare you for how overwhelming this can become. There are a lot of factors that can be considered, like if you're coaching full-time, what the average income is of the athletes that you are targeting, and if you have the reputation and experience to charge a higher fee. The list can go on and on.

Free is an option (WARNING!) but I have learned that coaching for free is not always easy. I'll put it this way—90% of the people that want free coaching give you 90% less of their effort. Simply put, people will use you. They have nothing invested, so they are not losing anything. Even if you are only charging $25, it's more likely that athletes will appreciate the services that you are providing. You can coach for free, but just accept what the risks are.

Then there's the other end of the spectrum. You want to charge $600 a month because you feel that's what you are worth, but you may be the only one that feels that way. Sorry. I know it sounds brutal, but believe me, it is very true. Just because you *can* charge anything doesn't mean you *should*. You will learn over time what works best for you through a little trial and error, and even though you can't just base your fees on what other coaches do, it's ok to research what they offer and why. You can even reach out to me if you'd like! The key is not to be too rigid. Over time you will find what works for you.

During your journey to become an amazing coach, things will not always be easy. In this chapter, I wanted to show you a few things that I had trouble with at the beginning, and some things I'm still working through. I couldn't tell you all the great things that come from coaching, but not also share the struggles that will pop up from time-to-time. Be prepared for anything to happen by educating yourself through other coaches' experiences. That's what makes an amazing coach—that ability to be resilient when other coaches give up. Allow mistakes to be the lessons that build your knowledge. Learning never stops, and you never know— maybe you will find a better way of doing things to share with the next generation of coaches. Use the hard times as a test of your resilience and you will always be prepared for the next obstacle.

10

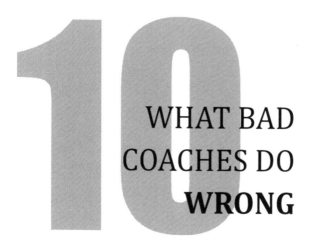

WHAT BAD COACHES DO WRONG

There are amazing coaches, and there are THEM. Yep, THEM.

O h my God. There are so many things I could tell you about bad coaches. Even while I've been writing this book, I have seen some questionable actions from a few coaches. A week prior to writing this chapter, while I was scrolling through my Facebook feed, I saw a conversation that a coach was having with a gentleman. It looked interesting, so I stopped scrolling to read all of the comments. I was taken aback by the language the coach was using to speak to this man (imagine the gentleman had cut the coach off in L.A. traffic and the coach responded before have a morning cup of coffee—harsh and very disrespectful). By the looks of the conversation, the coach didn't seem to even know him. I thought to myself, "This is the type of coach that gives coaches a bad name."

During this chapter I will show you how the bad coaches do it wrong. Coaching is not rocket science, but some miss the mark entirely on doing it right. Who you are as a person will really determine the type of coach you will become—a coach that works for the athletes or a coach that works only for self.

Bad Coaches Don't Make the Athlete's Life a Priority

When a coach (that an athlete is spending their hard-earned money on) thinks that what they want is more important than what the athlete needs, this can become problematic. In my opinion, no athlete can truly benefit from this type of ego-driven approach to coaching. Yes, there will be many occasions where the coach will need to explain why they need the athlete to do a certain thing, but this should be for the betterment of the athlete—not the coach.

If a coach is not taking the time to understand all the circumstances around the athlete's personal and professional commitments, they will have a difficult time building a plan that works best for the athlete. The coach needs to consider, for instance, if the athlete works eight to twelve hours on any given day or if the athlete's divorce decree dictates that they will have their kids every other weekend. These two factors alone would change the dynamics of the coach's approach. What we don't want to do as coaches is add extra stress (other than training stress) to the athlete's current situation.

For many athletes, the sport that they are involved in is just a hobby. If that hobby becomes the thing that disrupts their career or family time, it will be the first thing that is cut when things get too challenging to maintain. You may be thinking that this sounds simple, but believe me; there are many athletes that have (or have had) coaches that don't understand how important an athlete's other commitments are to their mental and physical well-being. There are many people that say, "The athlete should make the time." Last I checked, one of the responsibilities of the coach was helping the athlete *find the structure* that works best for them.

Bad coaches don't incorporate an athlete's whole life. However, if you put the needs of the athlete first (like family time or understanding long work hours) you will be the coach they respect and not the coach they run from. When you keep the line of communication open, you will be able to have conversations with your athletes that will benefit your athlete-coach relationship. Each athlete's success depends greatly on your willingness to understand them as a person.

Bad Coaches Avoid Difficult Conversations

As valuable as communication is, it can be tarnished if not handled properly. There will be many occasions when you will have to have conversations with your athletes that will not be easy for either of you. This is a part of coaching that cannot be avoided, though many have tried. Coaches and athletes will sometimes avoid even general communication when there is a topic or concern that is uncomfortable for them. This practice can really hurt a coach's reputation and prevent the athlete from seeing the progress they are looking for. I believe, and tell my athletes on the regular, that doing the right thing is sometimes the hardest thing to do.

An athlete may not want to hear that they shouldn't participate in an upcoming event on their schedule, but does that mean you shouldn't have that conversation just because you don't want to make them feel bad? You have to have this conversation because they could get hurt or have such a bad experience that they just stop participating in events altogether.

The hard stuff needs to be addressed. You, as the coach, have a responsibility to provide any and all information that could impact the athlete's success. Trying to circumvent this process in any way can lead to disaster. Most athletes understand that their coach needs to do this, but there are some that have never experienced it. They have been with coaches that told them only what they wanted to hear—they haven't experienced an amazing coach yet. When you run across these athletes, you have to be very mindful of how you deliver the hard information. Remember that they haven't been told the truth very often, so they are not expecting it, and may not know how to handle it. Be understanding. A coach never, by any means, gets a pass to be mean or harsh. Good communication and honesty still need to be practiced with respect.

Bad Coaches Don't Show Athletes Respect

I have heard many stories about coaches being very disrespectful toward their athletes. This is not a small issue; that's why this issue has to be addressed. Being disrespectful is **never** acceptable in any case, and it is surely not acceptable when you are doing it to someone that has asked for your help. I had one athlete share with me that a coach told them, "You will never be good at running, so you should find another sport." I was amazed and heartbroken that a **coach** would speak to an athlete this way. On another occasion I had an athlete share that a coach told them, "You will never be able to do an Ironman—you should stop trying." I was thinking to myself that there is no way a **coach** would say that.

During my time as a coach I have heard a lot of stories like these, and sometimes even worse. Like this one for example... During a running event, the coach said, "That was a slow run. You should go back to the start and shoot yourself with the starting pistol." I was like, *WHAT?! Did I hear what I just thought I heard?* The old saying, "Treat people like you want to be treated" is right. Absolutely no one deserves to be disrespected, no matter what their physical, mental, or emotional abilities are.

As coaches we should always set the example. Everything we say and do is a direct reflection of who we are. Respect is how we show people how much we value them—a lack of respect represents the total opposite. Also remember that being a disrespectful coach will prevent you from truly getting to know your athletes.

Bad Coaches Don't Get to Know an Athlete

What a lot of coaches fail to understand is that the word *athlete* is merely a title. Though some of your athletes will try to let this title define them, it's not who they actually are. First and foremost, we are all human beings. Athletes are also mothers and fathers, wives and husbands, sisters and brothers, friends, employees, and neighbors. This means that there will be other responsibilities in the athlete's life the coach will need to account for.

Let's start with this question. How are you able to effectively coach an athlete that you know nothing about? You can't. (The key word, for those looking to play in the gray area here, is **effectively**.) Sure, you can give the athlete a workout schedule, but is that going to be effective if the athlete has limitations or schedule conflicts that you know nothing about? To think that there are coaches out there that say, "I don't need to know the athlete's personal business," or my favorite, "The athlete needs to figure it out." Are you kidding me? I wonder what would happen if one of these bad coaches asked someone for help and they were told to "figure it out." I am pretty sure they wouldn't like that one bit.

Being able to understand the athlete's needs can only happen when the coach takes the time to get to know the athlete. A good coach will ask more questions. An amazing coach will really take the time to get to know the athlete as a person. A bad coach will leave it up to the athlete to figure it out on their own. To discount what the athlete has going on in life is to limit what the athlete can accomplish. Be the coach that sees your athletes for who they are, and your athletes will always see how important they are to you.

You and you alone will determine what type of influence you have on an athlete. As a coach, you are also a leader and people will look to you to set an example daily. From this, they will decide what they should or shouldn't do. Make your actions pure, fair, and consistent, and your athletes will find the best versions of themselves. Who you are as a person will really determine the type of coach you will become. Learn about your athletes, respect them, be honest with them even when it feels uncomfortable, and most of all, make the athlete a priority. Strive, in *every* moment, to be an amazing coach and you will put the coaches who are doing it wrong out of business.

NEW COACH STARTER KIT

Learning is great, but there is nothing wrong with a head start.

While we're usually excited about new jobs or new careers, we're often not ready for them. We just get thrown in. Wouldn't it be nice to be given a starter kit? Wouldn't it be nice to be given the tools to be successful? Most of the time we're just expected to figure it out. Sometimes we might have people that point us in the right direction, but the answers can still be vague and leave us feeling like we don't really understand what direction to go. We want specifics!

So in this chapter, I want to give you a *New Coach Starter Kit*. Go ahead—I'll wait for the applause to die down.

I know this is super exciting. You're probably thinking, "Morgon! This is such a great idea!" I know, right?! Seriously, though... At one point, I was right where you are. I want to give you things I wish somebody had given me at the beginning of my coaching career. I had to learn the hard way. Sometimes the hard way is necessary to learn, but in this case, you can learn from my mistakes. You can circumvent the hard way and spend that time really building your business and taking care of your athletes by being an amazing coach.

Some of the topics I'm most commonly asked about include

- specifics on insurance
- how I organize schedules for my athletes
- how I communicate with my athletes
- branding
- all about marketing (how to find people that will hire you)

In this chapter, I am going to answer all of those questions for you, so whatever you do, don't stop reading! I'm about to blow your mind.

Just kidding. This is just basic information, but I want you to have it. So, let's get to it...

Insurance

Should I have insurance?

Yes. On top of being very important, having insurance makes you feel validated in a way. It makes you feel like your coaching will be taken more seriously.

To start, let's go back to the idea of coaching a friend or family member. This comes with less liability. What does that mean? It means it's less likely that these people are going to use the *American Way* on you and sue your butt. But it's not completely out of the question... So, even with those closest to you, if there's even a **slight** chance they would take you to court, how are you going to protect yourself? How do you cover your family, your assets, and the things that are generally important to you? Insurance.

Insurance is not even that expensive! There are multiple companies you can use. (I'm not going to give you any names here because I don't endorse any companies. Plus, what's good for me might not be as good for you. It's best to do your own research.) Find companies that insure coaches, swim coaches, personal trainers, or people generally within the fitness industry. A solid insurance policy usually runs around $200-$400 annually, depending on the kind of coverage you get.

What size policy do I need?

I've noticed that when I use facilities or I am at events, they usually require at least $1 million worth of coverage. I'm ambitious, so I went with $3 million worth of coverage. Plus, I want to make **sure** that nobody tries to take everything I have. Do I have $3 million worth of stuff? Nope! But none of my assets are getting touched. You might need more. You might need less. This is a good baseline though. Make sure that you meet any criteria the facility or event has for providing insurance coverage. Then make sure that any insurance policy you get will cover the things that are most valuable to you. Super simple, right?

Is insurance from a governing body such as USAT enough?

Some certification governing bodies will provide insurance just for their coaches.

For example, I'm a U. S. Masters Swimming coach. As long as I'm coaching U. S. Masters Swimming members, I'm covered under their coaching plan and their coaching policy. If I'm coaching non-members, their policy isn't valid for me. There are a lot of organizations out there like that—just make sure you understand the limits of the coverage offered, and know if your athletes will fall under that policy. If they don't, consider some additional insurance.

———————

Alright. So we've talked about covering the liabilities of coaching, but that means we needs athletes to coach! No athletes equal no liabilities, but that's no fun. No athletes really equal no money to pay for insurance. So how do we get athletes?

Marketing

Is there one best way to market myself?

No. The only important thing is to make athletes aware of you. If athletes don't know who you are, they can't hire you. Simple. However, as you think about putting your name out there, it's helpful to know which platforms you're well-versed in. Some coaches prefer increasing athletes' awareness solely with social media, and some coaches prefer going to races and getting their name out there in person. Some coaches even prefer using local media (newspaper or radio) to get their names out.

There are a lot of places to get your name out there, but I want you to remember this—you need to understand the demographics of the people you want to coach. So if you want to coach a younger crowd, you'll probably find them on Instagram. If you want to target more middle-aged people, you'll probably find them on Facebook. If you're looking to coach seniors, it's less likely you'll find them on social media at all, and more likely they'll be looking in places like the newspaper or the local radio. Word of mouth works across the board, regardless of the platform. Thinking about these aspects will help you.

It's also important to remember that the best marketing can come from your athletes. The better their experience is with you, the more they are going to tell other people about you. It's like a wildfire—the more you feed it, the faster (and farther) it will spread with your name in it.

"My coach is amazing! He's awesome at communication."

"My coach really looks at my training data and takes the time to analyze it."

"My coach is super honest with me—he just gets me."

"My coach is a great dancer." (Awkward.)

You want to rock their world—in a coaching sense, of course—so your athletes will be your best ambassadors. This is why I recommend that you invest about 90% of your time into your athletes. Their experience with you will echo throughout the endurance community.

How much should I pay for marketing?

Cost is important. And the best cost is? SAY IT FROM THE BOTTOM! Free. Free is awesome. Try to find different ways to get your name out there for free, and a lot of financial stress can be alleviated for you as you are starting your coaching career.

I'd recommend, however, that as you start to grow, you start investing into varied platforms as ways to improve your reach and to grow your presence in whatever coaching community you are involved in.

Become an AMAZING Coach

Okay, you have the athletes, you're covered by insurance... Now what? You have to find a good way to communicate with them! You **have** to.

Athlete Communication

What is the best way to keep in touch with athletes?

Whatever works best for you and is consistent. You need to designate a certain platform for communication with your athletes. Just within your smart phone, you have so many things to choose from. You have Facebook messenger, text messages, WhatsApp, email, etc.

I personally prefer text messages and Facebook messenger. Most of my athletes come to me through Facebook, so messenger is easy because they are already on there. Texting works because we're all on our phones texting family and friends throughout the day already. You can also create groups where communication can happen between you and multiple (or all of your) athletes.

There are a lot of ways to set up this communication. Be creative, but do what's best for you. It's easy to say, "I want to do what works best for each athlete," but I'm going to tell you now that every athlete has different communication preferences. While you need to be well-versed in different modes of communication, you also need to be able to respectfully tell an athlete which mode of communication works best for you. The bottom line is that you need a line of communication open between you and your athletes to make it easier for them to be open with you.

All this communication is great, but what will you talk about, exactly? You have to talk about scheduling, training plans, data, progress, etc. How are you planning on delivering the athlete's training? How are you giving them feedback? You want athletes to accomplish their goals and strive to be healthier and fitter, so you need a good platform for all of this as well.

Schedules & Data

How should I track schedules and data for my athletes?

You can use a scheduling program, a spreadsheet, a simple e-mail, or you can even mail handwritten copies of the plan (I don't actually recommend this last one). So many new coaches (hell, even veteran coaches) make this too difficult. They think they need to be on a certain platform. Nope. The important thing is to find what works best for you, because once you do that, the delivery process to the athlete will be a lot simpler.

Don't complicate things. For instance, if you're not a super technical person, don't spend time or money trying to use a certain scheduling program that you don't fully understand. If it's complicated to you, how are you going to use it to explain anything to your athletes? Keep it simple. If you can easily understand the system, you can easily explain things to your athletes. Everyone is happy.

———

Everything so far leads to one final thing: Who are you? What is your brand?

Your Brand

What should I think about when I'm creating my brand?

I like this part. I like to be geared up and representing my brand. I really like seeing other people branding themselves too. Creating that logo or that brand really helps foster team spirit. Create a simple logo that can go on all of your gear, or on anything at all.

You have to project out—think beyond where you are right now. Does that logo look good on a suitcase? You may be saying, "Morgon. I don't need suitcases. That's crazy." You say these things now, but when the opportunity to represent your brand on a bigger scale presents itself, you should take it. The more people that see your brand, the more people that know who you are. Create your logo, and you won't have to continue to wear somebody else's.

It's such a wonderful feeling to see other people wearing my logo and to see them representing my coaching company and our coaching family. A logo can give you that sense of ownership over what you're trying to create and the brand you're building. It's things like these that will always give you a sense of pride, show you how many lives you've touched, and remind you of how far you've come. Once you get here, you will have established your identity within the coaching community.

Sit down and organize the way you want things done, and figure out the way things will work for you; it will be time well spent in the beginning. You might even be able to find people close to you that already know how to help with certain things on this start-up list—take that help. Then you can go be that amazing coach I know you will be.

12
WHAT IT TAKES TO BE AN **AMAZING** COACH

When your heart is truly in the right place, anything is possible.

I think about what it takes to be an amazing coach a lot. I think about this so much that it has actually engulfed my way of thinking on a regular basis, and I think that it's been a vital part of my growth.

My goal is bigger than myself. My goal is to redefine how everyone else pictures themselves. I don't want to be a *good* coach.

I don't want to be an *alright* coach. I want to be an AMAZING coach. I want my athletes to say that I'm amazing. I want them to say, "He's changed my life. He's helped me do things that I didn't think I could do." I want to be able to show my athletes (or anybody I come into contact with) that they already possess everything they need to grow. But in order to do that, I must (as a mentor, leader, and coach) understand growth in general.

The only way to truly understand something is to go through it yourself, and to figure it out. Everybody is different and not everybody's growth is going to happen in the same way, but it's the same general foundation, right? You can't tell someone else that something is possible when you've never explored the possibilities yourself. It's just not going to happen.

The first part of being an amazing coach (or even just a good coach!) is complete dedication to what you're trying to accomplish. That's the most important thing. It becomes a huge portion of your life in the sense that it overtakes the way that you think—everything you do or say becomes a part of your dedication to the task.

For me, I want people to feel amazing and be amazing. I want them to feel emotionally, spiritually, and physically amazing with who they are. That means I have to learn to feel amazing and be amazing too.

So how do I grow, and how do I affect someone else's growth in the same way? How do I become the amazing coach that I'm looking to be and give the people around me the things that I'm looking to give them?

Educate Yourself First

I take time to educate *myself* first. I make it a point to read as much as possible and to speak to other coaches/colleagues and other athletes as much as possible, because the only way for me to be an amazing coach for others is to truly gather as much information as I can. It's like being an encyclopedia of people. I get information from here, from there, and from everywhere, then I take that information and allow it to help me build relationships with the people around me. With my athletes, and generally with the people around me that really mean something to me. Not only does this stuff affect how I deal with my athletes, it also affects my relationships with my mother, my father, my significant other, my kids, my brother and my sister. Becoming an amazing coach helps me transition into being an amazing human being.

Learn How to Listen

I learned how to listen and to hear what's being said without being told. And I know that's some deeper stuff, but bear with me here. Being able to hear what's being said without being told is this: sometimes people say things, but what they *mean* is totally different. Their body language might be different, or the way they present things might be different from their actual words. Learn how to listen to the messages that aren't spoken.

Be an Amazing Human Being

I've learned to constantly seek to possess the traits to be an amazing human being. I have to be empathetic. I have to be compassionate. I have to be honest. I have to be loyal. That's what being an amazing human being is about, right? I also have to possess courage, and enthusiasm, and honor, and commitment to a task. There are so many things that I need to possess as a human being before I can be an amazing coach.

Look Inside Yourself

You see a lot of people out there saying they want to be this amazing coach, but they're not also trying to be amazing people. They're just trying to live inside a title, but they don't understand that the title connects to who they are. This isn't easy for everyone— not everybody can look inside and make changes. It can take time. But introspection gives you the ability to know what you need to fix.

As I grow relationships with my athletes, I listen to them. I pay attention to what they say, do, and think. Because while the way they view me is not usually the way I view myself, I'd actually venture to say that the way they view me probably reflects more honestly about who I really am. They're going to see things that I don't see. It's like when we have nervous tics that we do, and we don't even see them. We've probably been doing them our whole lives, but when someone points it out it's like, "Man! I didn't even know I did that!" Or, "I didn't even know I said that or did things that way!"

If I stop focusing on what I think I already know and allow myself to understand that there is so much I don't know, then my athletes will not only learn from me, but I can learn from them. They will feel that. I will be that conduit of good and positive information that I want to be for them, but they will also know that they are valued by me, because I learn from them as well. I'm not talking about financial value. I'm talking about an emotional, mental, and spiritual value that happens when you have a good relationship with anyone. The energy is felt between both of you. You just feel like you are in the right place, with the right spiritual connection, and at the right time with the right person. That's how you can resonate with others and become an amazing coach and an amazing human being.

It's About Relationships

By first growing yourself, you are able to confidently express yourself to people because you have taken the time, and had the patience, to learn what you don't know. And you've allowed other people in your life to share how they feel about you so you can improve on who you are.

Certifications don't make you amazing. Your education doesn't make you amazing. These things just make you educated or make you knowledgeable. What makes an amazing coach is the relationship that you are able to have with any given person at any given time. If you find an amazing coach, you'll see that they resonate with their athletes, with their athlete's family, with their athlete's friends, and with their own family, because they possess things that make them great human beings.

Don't Hold Yourself Back

It's not about dictating workouts, or managing expectations, or anything like that. It's about making an athlete see what they're capable of by showing them what they already possess. When you show somebody something so emotionally attached to who they are and to their growth, and you show them not just where they've come from but where they're capable of going, they will think you're amazing. They will feel in their heart that you are the person that should be coaching them. But you can only do this if you are able to first do it for yourself.

The moral of all of this is don't hold back. Don't bottle up who you are. Learn about yourself and all you are capable of. Allow yourself to be who you truly are, because the way you are will attract the type of people that will connect with you the best. If you're not being your best self, your **true** self, you will attract people who are nothing like you and the relationships are probably going to be trash.

I've always heard (and have always said) that the truth will set you free. If you're honest with yourself and are willing to do the work of self-growth, others will realize that, and they will be honest and truthful with you as well. They will trust you with their personal development. And if you're able to get the honesty and the truth from the people you're trying to influence, then you'll be able to get something out of them that they're not even able to get out of themselves.

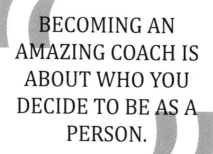

BECOMING AN AMAZING COACH IS ABOUT WHO YOU DECIDE TO BE AS A PERSON.

Becoming an amazing coach is not all about technical skill. It's about who you decide to be as a person and how that person affects the world. That's how I see being an amazing coach. What are you going to do now? Hit me up.

Conclusion

I'm so proud that you have made it to the conclusion of this book. Though the book is coming to its end, your journey has just begun. You have read how impactful the coaching experience truly is, and you have also read about some of the challenges that will come with becoming an amazing coach. I'll be the first to tell you (if you don't already know by now), that it is worth it. This journey has changed me inside and out, and it will do the same for you. In hard times, be resilient; in good times, cherish every moment. Most people will never know what it's like to have a positive impact on someone's life, but after taking the leap of becoming a coach, you will not have that problem.

To make a lasting and amazing impact, I am going to give you a list of things to do (or think about). Most conclusions just sum up what the book's main points are and then say good luck. I want to provide an easy reference for you so you won't have to go back through the book just to get the key points you need to be successful. Below, you will find some key points and questions that I feel will keep you on track.

1
Amazing Coach Wisdom 1:

The ability to honestly look within is not a trait possessed by everyone, so give yourself credit for that. Remember, the foundation you lay at the beginning will be the support for the relationships you have with your athletes (and others) for years to come. Look inside yourself before starting this journey.

Question: Are your emotional, mental, and physical fitness in a good place for you to help others, or is there work to do on yourself first?

2 Amazing Coach Wisdom 2:

Your journey of self-growth will teach you that you can be a part-time coach and also a husband, a wife, a sister, an employee, or whatever else is important to you. You can be awesome at more than one thing—you just have to make intentional choices about what those things will be. Avoid over-filling your plate, and work to find your harmony.

Question: What processes will you put in place to ensure you don't take on too many responsibilities?

3 Amazing Coach Wisdom 3:

Getting started in coaching takes some work. You've got to be willing to put in the time and effort to sort out the details. Full-time coaching comes after important steps are taken. There are coaches that will not take any of these steps, and you will see them pass through coaching like a season.

Question: Have you decided on how to get organized, what the structure of your coaching will be, and how you will handle your finances?

Amazing Coach Wisdom 4:

There are going to be many times in your life when you have to "just get started." Your coaching career starts with just one person. Just one friend in your corner, and just one belief that something really big can happen if you do it right.

Question: Have you focused on finding **one** person that will allow you to coach them for one event?

Amazing Coach Wisdom 5:

Don't sell yourself, or your journey, short because you are fearful of the unknown. Cut out the negative self-talk. It's natural to want to be the best at everything you do, but you don't have to be *the best*. You just have to be willing to do **your** best.

Question: Are you coaching with your passion to help people, or with your fear of not being good enough?

6

Amazing Coach Wisdom 6:

Believe in yourself and your ability to impact others. Stop holding yourself back. Know better, do better, be better. You have everything it takes to impact so many lives—choose to use it.

Question: Do you remember that you are here to have a positive impact on someone's life?

7

Amazing Coach Wisdom 7:

Having a mentor coach throughout your entire career—not just at the beginning—is important. Everybody has the ability to continue learning. You just have to have an open enough mind to hear different points of view—even if you never agree with them.

Question: Have you selected a mentor that will challenge you to be an amazing coach?

Morgon Latimore

8
Amazing Coach Wisdom 8:

Be prepared for anything to happen by educating yourself through other coaches' experiences. That's what makes an amazing coach—the ability to be resilient when other coaches give up. Allow mistakes to be the lessons that build knowledge.

Question: Are you building your coaching knowledge so that you are prepared for anything?

9
Amazing Coach Wisdom 9:

You, and you alone, will determine what type of influence you have on an athlete. As a coach, you are also a leader. People will look to you to set the example daily. You can be an amazing coach by first being an amazing person.

Question: Are you setting an example you would want your athletes to emulate?

Final Thoughts

I'll finish this book how I started it. You are needed, and this book is for you. Don't waste your gifts. There is one person out there right now who is waiting for what you have to offer. Their journey can begin the moment you decide to become an AMAZING COACH!

Additional Reading

Brown, Brene. 2012. *Daring Greatly: How the Courage to be Vulnerable Transforms the Way we Live, Love, Parent and Lead.* New York: Gotham.

Coelho, Paulo. 2020. *The Alchemist.* United States: Harper.

Coleman, Joey. 2018. *Never Lose a Customer Again.* New York: Penguin Putnam.

Gladwell, Malcolm. 2011. *The Tipping Point: How Little Things Can Make a Big Difference.* London: Little, Brown and Company.

Harris, Dan. 2019. *10% Happier.* New York: HarperCollins.

McKeown, Greg. 2014. *Essentialism.* London: Ebury.

Sinek, Simon. 2011. *Start with Why.* New York: Penguin Putnam.

Vaynerchuk, Gary. 2018. *Crushing It!* New York: HarperCollins.

About Morgon *"The Peoples Coach"* Latimore

Morgon is an empowerment speaker, IRONMAN certified coach, and career Marine with over 21 years of experience teaching personal and leadership development. He specializes in designing and delivering employee engagement sessions, giving internal teamwork and leadership training workshops, presenting motivational seminars for schools and youth organizations, recording voice-overs, and endurance coaching.

For more information about any of these services, contact Morgon:

- Endurance Coaching
- Coach Mentoring
- Virtual Speaker (i.e. ZOOM)
- Empowerment Speaker
- Life Coaching

Email: CoachMorgon@LPureCoaching.com

Instagram: @coachmorgonlatimore

Facebook: @peoplescoach

LinkedIn: @morgonlatimore

Made in the USA
Columbia, SC
11 September 2020